The Gray Flannel Tramp Constrained

Written By
MAURICE K. ISAAC

Illustrated By
MATTHEW E. ISAAC

Published by Eye of Infinity.
Printed by Lulu Press, Inc.

ISBN: 978-1-5136-3315-2

First Printing.

The
Gray Flannel Tramp
Constrained

Written By
Maurice K. Isaac

Illustrated By
Matthew E. Isaac

EYE OF INFINITY   GRAY FLANNEL TRAMP

Dedicated to

The memory of Donna Loomis,
my most loyal fan.

Contents

Foreword

"The Gray Flannel Tramp Constrained" refers to the constraints of poetic form. I explore the possibilities of several well known, time tested, poetic forms and also some lesser known foreign forms that present particular challenges when written in English. I have even developed a new form which I call "Prima al quadrato," partly inspired by dipping into the "**Oulipo★ Compendium**" and partly to while away hours spent in the plaza in Santa Fe.

I enjoy the challenge and satisfaction that comes with learning a new form and using it in a personal and unconventional way. For example, I have been able to express my love for both rugby and opera in several different poetic forms. What began as an exercise has become a passion and, far from constraining me, writing within a set of rules has freed me to concentrate on content.

My feelings about free verse are aptly summed up by W. H. Auden, "The poet who writes 'free' verse is like Robinson Crusoe on his desert island: he must do all his cooking, laundry and darning for himself. In a few exceptional cases, this manly independence produces something original and impressive, but more often the result is squalor – dirty sheets on the unmade bed and empty bottles on the unswept floor." While not obssessively clean and tidy, I do like things to be "ship shape and Bristol fashion," and so constraints of poetic form are, for me, a framework and a discipline within which I flourish.

Maurice K Isaac
Houston
July 2017

★**Oulipo** (French pronunciation ulipo), short for *Ouvroir de littérature potentielle*; roughly translated: "*work-shop of potential literature*" is a loose gathering of (mainly) French-speaking writers and mathematicians who seek to create works using constrained writing techniques.

The
Gray Flannel Tramp
Constrained

SONNETS

The sonnet is probably the best-known poetic form of all. So common in fact that the term sonneteer is mildly derogatory. Whole books have been written about sonnets and almost every famous poet has tried their hand at writing them. There are even sonnets about writing sonnets! For these reasons I will give only the simplest description of the form.

A sonnet has 14 lines, divided into two sections: normally an octave (or octet) followed by a sestet. Often the octave will pose a question that the sestet answers; or the two sections will put contrasting points of view. The main differences between Petrarchan, Spenserian, Shakespearean, etc sonnets are the rhyming scheme.

I started out with the assumption that sonnets should be about love, but have since concluded that one can write a sonnet on just about any subject. Fourteen lines seem just sufficient to express an opinion, describe a thing of beauty, make a point or raise a smile. I find that sonnets are my "Go To" form and have included examples on a wide range of topics.

RUGBY MAIDENS

Unshielded maidens, modern amazons,
In shorts and studded boots, hair tightly bound,
Who use the rugby field as combat zone,
Your rougeless faces red with blood and mud,
Heaving in scrums and rolling mauls you fight,
Self serving Valkyrie who raise your own,
Not to Valhalla, but to sporting heights,
Undreamed by milder sisters clad in gowns.
Do you sing risque songs and drink warm beer,
Cavort, in locker room and steamy shower,
Indulge in horseplay, comrades for ever,
Relive hard tackles, tries, that sense of power.
Then, freshly scrubbed, shake out your pony tails,
Put on new mask to cast your female spells?

GAY MARRIAGE

Towards "gay" marriage I'm ambivalent.
Perhaps it's nature's way to circumvent
Malthusian over population threats.
For hetero union alone begets
Those pesky children, who will overrun
Our planet, be the death of everyone,
Consume the food and breath the oxygen,
Make obscene fortunes for the oilmen.
In infancy a wild fecundity,
To populate the earth, was necessary.
But now, to save it, childlessness is good,
And so our old morality we should
Revise, and recognize the greater worth
Of couplings that do not result in birth.

AIR BAG

Last night my airbag smacked me in the face.
I hit the curb a glancing blow. My fault !
I probably deserved this fall from grace.
If it had been my lady who had caught
Me in some situation indiscrete,
I could accept such sharp correction wrought
Upon my person in a flash of heat,
As penance for illicit pleasures sought.
But for a government mandated bag,
To save me from my own incompetence,
A nanny granny state officious nag,
To strike me with unwonted violence,
Stirs my resentment and rings out a curse.
It also tests the limits of my purse.

APRIL IS THE YELLOWEST MONTH IN SCOTLAND

Spring's golden rainbow glows prismatic yellow,
Gorse grades to broom and dancing daffodil.
Slip sliding cows munch buttercups and bellow.
Pale pastel primroses damp hedgerows fill.
Dandy the lion heads with hundred petals.
Bright fields of rapeseed promise yellow oil.
Celandines bloom as returning swallows,
With mud, on summer homes begin to toil.
This spectrum, just two hundred angstroms wide,
Has beauty that we struggle to express,
Without exemplars plucked from natures pride.
So minerals, flowers, fauna, fruit, we press
To serve as language of our lexicon,
Chrome and primrose, blond, canary, lemon.

UPON THE PRICK OF NOON

No longer do I feel the needle's prick,
Small price to pay to stay alive and well.
Three thousand times a year myself I stick,
Postpone the tolling of the Tailor's bell.
From conscience prick I finally am free.
No evil comes with pricking of my thumbs.
I fear no holy Bishopric's decree.
To prick of thorns my thickening skin is numb.
My seedlings having safely been pricked out,
I prick fresh patterns for my final days.
Convention's bubble prick, correctness flout,
Prick pomegranate seeds, the piper's paid.
My ears are pricked to hear the summoning drum,
*When called, **upon the prick of noon**, I'll come.*

VILLANELLE

The Villanelle started as a simple ballad-like song with no fixed form; this fixed quality would only come much later, from the poem "Villanelle (J'ay perdu ma Tourterelle)" (1606) by Jean Passerat. From this point, its evolution into the "fixed form" used in the present day is debated. Despite its French origins, the majority of Villanelles have been written in English, a trend which began in the late nineteenth century.

A villanelle is composed of five tercets followed by a quatrain. The first and last lines of the first tercet are repeated alternately as the last lines of the next four tercets and as the last two lines of the quatrain. There are only two rhymes; aba for each tercet and abaa for the quatrain.

Probably the most famous Villanelle in the English language is "Do not go gentle into that good night" by Dylan Thomas.

VILLANELLE FOR THE EARTH

Still steady on its axis spins the earth,
And still it rushes headlong round the sun,
While prophecies of doom are without worth.

For Spring remains the season of rebirth,
When all is fresh and green, and life begun,
And steady on its axis spins the earth.

While Summer still brings happiness and mirth,
Long days of playing in the surf are fun,
And prophecies of doom are without worth.

Then Autumn's harvest doth increase our girth,
So after feasting we are forced to run,
Though steady on its axis spins the earth.

Cruel Winter is the season when a dearth
Of fuel reminds us, without warmth we're done,
Still prophecies of doom are without worth.

Though glaciers may calve in child-birth,
In St Moritz there's still the Cresta Run,
Forever on its axis spins the earth,
And prophecies of doom are without worth.

WE OMNIVORES

Thank God whose wisdom made us omnivores.
Fish, meat and greens, eggs, dairy, we consume.
Till offal, fat, our failing strength restores.

Rejoice! fish roe, sheep's eyes, those reservoirs
Of cultural food can make our taste buds bloom,
Thank God whose wisdom made us omnivores.

Fat years when nature from its bounty pours
Are juxtaposed to lean, starvation looms,
Till offal, fat, our failing strength restores.

In times of struggle, hardship, and World Wars,
All dietary fads we will subsume.
Thank God whose wisdom made us omnivores.

When starving eat what every man abhors,
The product of a fellow human's womb
Till offal, fat, our failing strength restores.

Taste every liver, kidney, and legume,
The time for abstinence is in the tomb.
Thank God whose wisdom made us omnivores.
So offal, fat, our failing strength restores.

SAN FRANCISCO, SAN ANDREAS

The City by the Bay knows how to play,
Historic, hilly, beautiful and gay,
Until the San Andreas has its day.

First Gaspar de Portola found the way,
Mission Dolores let the Catholics pray,
And City by the Bay began to play.

In eighteen forty six, a brief affray,
And Yerba Buena then became passe,
Still San Andreas had not yet its day.

Then San Francisco built the great Broadway,
And every vice, and cardsharp, came to stay,
The City by the Bay learned how to play.

Nineteen-o-six, a year of great dismay,
City destroyed, in flames, doomsday,
But for the San Andreas not the day.

Though ancient Damoclean threat may lay,
Silent beneath our feet, still let us pray,
The City by the Bay knows how to play,
Until the San Andreas has its DAY.

THE RONDEAU

The Rondeau first appeared in France. Its name and form derive from the French *rondel*, which comes from the French *rond* ("round"). There, from the late 13th century into the 15th century, poetry of this form was often set to music.

Form.

In a traditional Rondeau, there are:

- 13, or 10, or 15 lines.
- Usually eight syllables in each line, except for the refrains, which have four syllables.
- Two rhymes.
- A refrain that repeats the *first* half (four syllables) of the first line. The refrain can also be considered to be a third rhyme.
- For 15 lines, the lines are grouped into:
  1. One quintet (5 lines rhyming a, a, b, b, a);
  2. One quatrain (4 lines rhyming a, a, b, plus refrain R);
  3. One sestet (6 lines rhyming a, a, b, b, a, (plus refrain R)

The secret to a good Rondeau is a memorable refrain. One of the best known Rondeau in the english language is "In Flander's Fields" by John McCrae.

31

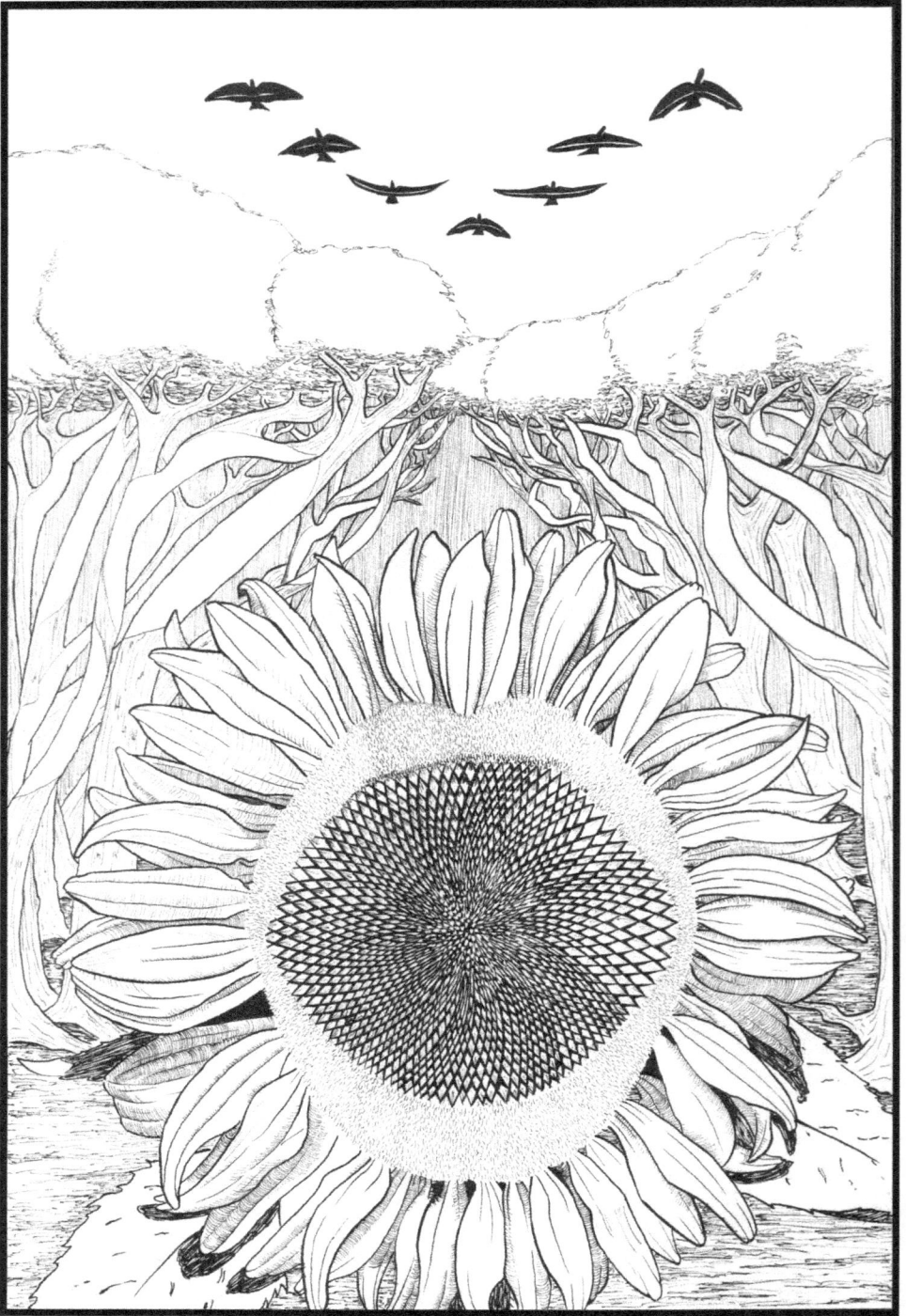

IF WE COULD HEAR

If we could hear the sunflowers sigh,
"The iceman comes our end is nigh,"
Would we confess we're powerless
Nature's imbalance to redress,
Too hot, too cold, we all must die.

In unison the forests cry,
"Your fear of CO2's a lie,
It is the key to our success,"
If we could hear.

The birds talk climate as they fly
Their pilgrimage to southern sky,
And polar bears their fears express,
"We hate this frozen wilderness,
We catch more seals when sea's nearby,"
If we could hear.

AFTER A RAIN

After a rain the cactus blooms.
Blossoms burst forth from prickled wombs.
Dry desert washes spring alive.
Forgotten flowers briefly thrive.
Erosion suddenly resumes.

New Orleans' coffins float from tombs,
Furnish fresh victims empty rooms,
Though most are tough and so survive,
After a rain.

Foul flood low neighborhoods subsumes
But stalwart Cajuns hide their glooms,
Down street canals their pirogues drive,
Save pets and people, dive by dive,
As fear of failing levees looms,
After a rain.

LIVING WITH DIABETES

Needles and blood, a daily trial,
Shots and carb counts cramping style.
Eat small meals become a shadow,
Meat and veggies but no sourdough,
A little rice once in a while.

Thank God I am no Francophile,
Living to eat a hard lifestyle,
Before a meal try not to show
Needles and blood.

Yet health obsession is worthwhile,
Without it life would soon be vile,
Nerve pain, blindness, worse to follow,
Coma could be final deathblow,
So sadly I must reconcile
Needles and blood.

THE BALLADE

The **Ballade** originated in France. It is a rhymed and syllabic form whose name derives from the Old French *balade* ("a dancing song").

François Villon (1431–1465?) wrote ballades, including Ballade des Dames du Temps Jadis, which has the famous refrain "Mais où sont les neiges d'antan?" ("But where are the snows of yesteryear?")

A **Ballade** has three 8-line stanzas rhyming ababbabA, followed by a 4-line envoi rhyming babA, the same rhymes being used throughout. The capital A's indicate that the same line is repeated at the end of each stanza as a refrain.

It was customary for the poet to address the envoi to his patron, or to someone referred to in the poem. These days, it is almost invariably addressed to "Prince". For some people this is "The Prince of Darkness", for me it is whoever fits the bill, my son, a real prince, an imagined patron.

I find this form good for comic poems with a message.

My favorite English **Ballade** is G. K. Chesterton's "A Ballade of Suicide".

THE UNWANTED JUROR

From civic duty I will not abstain,
I'll serve as juror, judge a man in court.
My dress is blazer, tie, for this campaign,
Show them I know a dumpling from a tort,
Make answers to their questions full not short.
But sadly all my efforts are in vain,
Lawyers dismiss my knowledge with a snort.
As juror I am peerless it is plain.

A year has passed and I will try again
To earn a jury seat the voir dire thwart.
This time no jacket, badly dressed and plain,
With commoners and hoi poloi consort.
A strategy of silence to support
My efforts to conceal my strong left brain.
Alas these lawyers recognize my sort.
As juror I am peerless it is plain.

Age limits my last call for jury fame,
By now I'm angry, feeling out of sorts.
I treat the whole proceeding with disdain,
Making no effort to impress the court.
Strangely, it seems this attitude comports
With just the kind of juror they retain,
Till "Chevron Oil, retired" they extort.
As juror I am peerless it is plain.

Envoi

Prince, from this cautionary tale take comfort,
For judgment of your peers is sought in vain,
Though juries, wise men fear and advocates distort,
As royalty you are peerless it is plain.

A BALLADE OF ARTIST'S LOST YOUTH

Our youthful minds drive bodies free of pain.
Each sight and sound and touch is new.
The sky's no limit, work is not in vain,
We still believe that promises come true.
We know our dreams of greatness will win through,
Filled with ideas to which we give free rein,
And do not ask old artists if they knew,
Why Monet painted lilies once again.

When experts criticize our work, disdain,
Delay our recognition, champagne too,
Undaunted then our genius we retrain,
Pour unproductive concepts down the loo.
As poverty, rejection, turn the screw,
Who cares when patron State our art sustains.
No need to fear that hoary bugaboo,
Why Monet painted lilies once again.

Eventually we sell a piece arcane,
A single buffalo on a plain of blue
Grass, under a sky that hints at rain.
"Despondent beast in bluish slue."
Now we are in the critics field of view,
We will with buffaloes blue good life sustain,
As finally we think we see right through
Why Monet painted lilies once again.

Envoi

But if my Prince you were his patron true
You'd know Monet could not his genius chain
For him each lily was forever new
So Monet painted lilies once again.

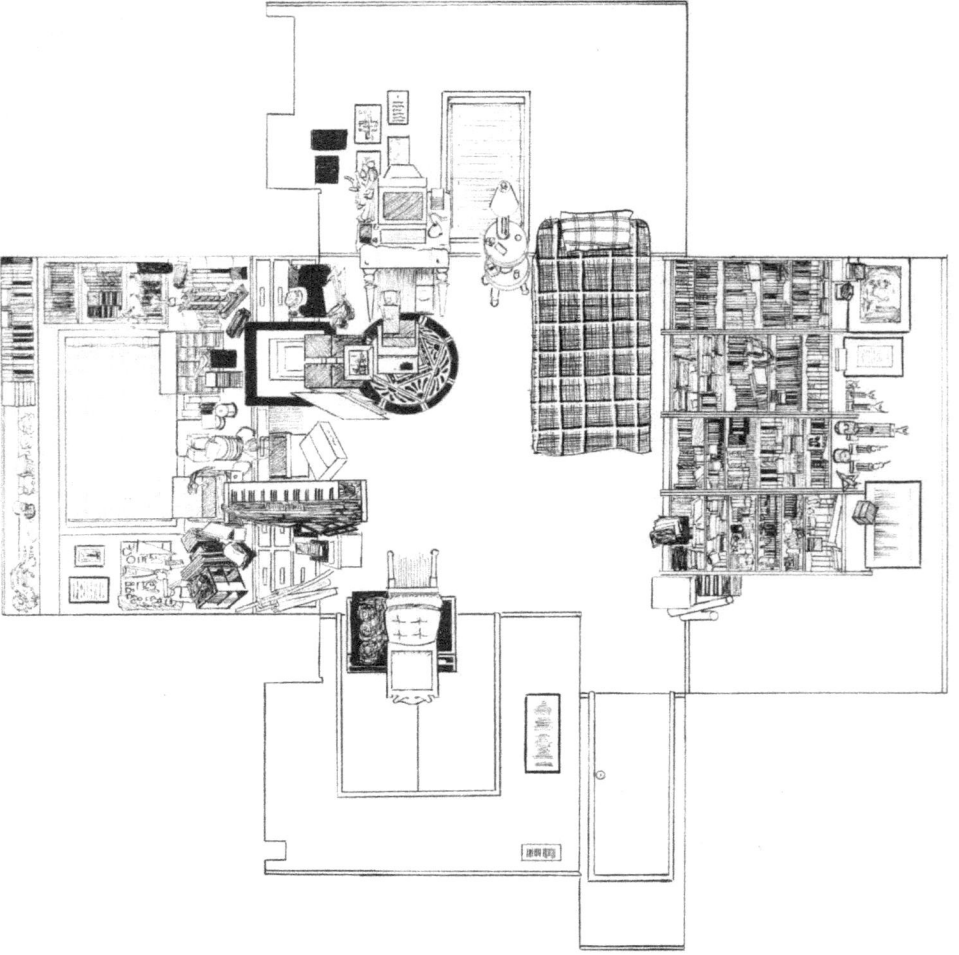

HIS ROOM

I thought it too untidy and ill kept,
Yet only in an absent minded way,
Had I into a jumbled time warp stepped,
Filled with strange artifacts from yesterday,
Odd dusty memories left there to decay.
Embarrassed, I would leave it long unswept,
My zealous cleaning ladies keep away,
But often now I boast "here's where he slept"

Eclectic library, for an adept
In subjects far to numerous to say.
I never dreamed the boundaries he'd leapt,
Until he called, and asked me to cherchez,
And find upon the shelves, without delay,
A volume critical to some precept.
My first reaction was surprised dismay,
But often now I boast "here's where he slept"

With sentiment I never would suspect,
On walls, shelves, floor, in random disarray,
Mementos, pictures, trophies he had kept.
A turntable, two keyboards he would play,
Old bolos and a gold etched china tray.
A mounted butterfly I could accept,
Found parasols and wooden sword outre.
But often now I boast "here's where he slept"

Envoi

Princeling, forgive if I, in pride, betray
The secrets of your room, or overstep
Your bounds and filial strictures disobey.
But often now I boast "here's where you slept"

THE PANTOUM

The pantoum is a Malay verse form that reached us via France. (The original Malay word is pantun, but the verse form of that name in present-day Malaysia is different from the one described here.)

The poem should have at least four quatrains, but could have more, with the rhyming scheme abab, bcbc, cdcd etc. The second and fourth lines of each stanza reappearing as the first and third lines of the next. To complete the loop, the second and fourth lines of the final stanza are usually the same as the third and first lines of the first stanza.

My first reaction was that a pantoum would be easy to write as there are so many repeated lines. In fact this is not true as there can be no enjambments (carry overs to the next line). Each line must stand alone and make sense in two places. For this reason some modern pantoums do not observe all the rules.

My favorite pantoum is Charles Baudelaire's "Harmonie du soir" both in the original and in translation.

BUFFALO BAYOU

Sad bayou, muddy, sluggish stream,
Flows strongly only after rain,
Home to the fish of Cajun dream,
Cat and sun and craw domain.

Flows strongly only after rain,
No buffalo wallowing its banks,
Cat and sun and craw domain.
Where herons, egrets, fish in ranks.

No buffalo wallowing its banks,
Houston's bayou is oddly named.
Where herons, egrets, fish in ranks,
But for it's flooding it was famed.

Houston's bayou is oddly named,
After the buffalo, mighty beast,
But for it's flooding it was famed,
Till earthen dams it's threat decreased.

After the buffalo, mighty beast,
Home to the fish of Cajun dream,
Till earthen dams it's threat decreased,
Sad bayou, muddy, sluggish stream.

EULOGISTIC WAVES

Sit spell bound on a shingle beach.
Time slows as each receding wave
Whispers a eulogistic speech,
For saints interred in watery grave.

Time slows as each receding wave,
Repeating sadly rasps its song
For saints interred in watery grave,
Sounds death march infinitely long.

Repeating sadly rasps its song,
Sighing to tell of loss and strife,
Sounds death march infinitely long,
In memory of a storm crossed life.

Sighing to tell of loss and strife,
Whispers a eulogistic speech
In memory of a storm crossed life.
Sit spell bound on a shingle beach.

THE END OF QEH

Centuries of proud tradition,
Bookended by Elizabeths,
Bend to feminist petition
To end a cherished shibboleth.

Bookended by Elizabeths,
Great Queens who would reluctant be
To end a cherished shibboleth,
Just for some false economy.

Great Queens who would reluctant be
To amend a charter royal,
Just for some false economy,
So confounding old boys loyal.

To amend a charter royal,
Bend to feminist petition,
So confounding old boys loyal
Centuries of proud tradition.

THE SESTINA

The **Sestina**, which was invented by a twelfth-century Provençal troubador, does not rhyme. It has six key-words essential to the poem's structure. The poem's 39 lines – six 6-line stanzas followed by a 3-line envoi or tornada – all end with one of the keywords in a prescribed, rotating, order; in the tornada, there are two keywords in each line, one of them at the end and the other somewhere in the middle.

I find this form useful for telling a story or driving home a point by the repetition of the six key words. For this reason I spend much of my time on the first stanza and the choice of line endings.

My favorite example of a **Sestina** is Ezra Pound's "Sestina: Altaforte" which was first published in June, 1909.

JUMBLED MEMORIES OF CHRISTMAS

Jumbled memories of a Merry Christmas
Unwrapping gifts, delicious dinner,
Ice-tinsel, cotton-snow and candle fire,
A cornucopia beneath the tree.
Child's paper chains our decoration,
Doors open for an urchin choir.

In Africa a Bulawayo choir,
Rhodesia merits Kipling Christmas,
Flood-lit trophy heads for decoration,
Toasting Queen and Rhodes at dinner,
Underneath baobab trees,
Brats roasting on an open fire.

Mountains aglow with golden fire,
Vibrating warbles of an oldster choir,
Battered ancient plastic tree,
Westward Ho for in-laws' Christmas.
Football before and after dinner,
Light up saguaros' decorations.

Snow, streets lit with rainbow decorations,
Torch bearing skiers paint the runs with fire.
Eat alone a Denny's Diner dinner,
Caroling singers in the lodge no choir.
White and joyful Colorado Christmas,
Skiing Aspen's slopes betwixt the trees.

Lop-sided, last-on-lot and cheapest tree,
Nola's hand-sewn decorations.
Thank God for AC, Houston Christmas,
Embroidered stockings hung by fire.
Heart sung to pieces in St Martin's choir,
Capon, goose or duck for dinner.

This year no cards, or booze with dinner,
Enjoy the symmetry of ersatz tree,
O Come Emmanuel and bless our choir.
Raise the cherished decorations,
Collect the wood for needless fire,
Make ready for teetotal Christmas.

Tune the choir, hang the decorations,
Cook the dinner and festoon the tree,
Turn AC on and light the fire, one more Merry Christmas.

DOOMED LOVE

Strong are the ties of kinship and of blood,
Yet more resilient are the bands of love,
Forged by a fiery glance across a room,
Annealed and hammered into shape by lust.
So when between two families there is strife,
Inevitable is the couple's doom.

Untimely, bloody, cruel and useless doom
For those who challenge family bonds of blood,
And generations torn apart by strife.
No Capulet a Montague may love,
No Montague for Capulet should lust,
Or meet unarmed within a common room.

No more should Hatfields or McCoys give room,
To fresh liaisons that might spell the doom
Of feuds, prolonged by stubbornness and lust,
That never die as long as blood for blood
Is more important than the power of love.
No end to violent reoccurring strife.

Only the young would dare oppose such strife,
In innocent besotted hearts make room,
Forgive past wrongs and substitute new love,
And in so doing risk a brutal doom,
For old vendettas only feed on blood,
And ancient hatreds magnify old lust.

The young pray love will overcome blood lust,
That innocence will put an end to strife.
A child conceived with intermingled blood
Will move the feuding hearts to give it room,
Divert the warring families from doom,
As generations gaze on it with love.

Mouth Montague, eyes Capulet, plead love,
Yet grandparents who cry not love, but lust,
In horror, see unwanted grandchild doom
Their bloody feud to death, maintain cruel strife,
With poison, dagger, in a cold dark tomb,
And innocent teenage sacrifice of blood.

And yet, their love may put an end to strife,
For petty lust and vengeance have no room,
When shamed by blood and unborn infant's doom.

GRASS BEFORE BREAKFAST

Where is the honour in a suit at law?
Give me the sudden clash of swords at dawn,
Or pistol shots and silk shirts drenched in blood.
Grass before breakfast or be always scorned.
So with this gauntlet I give thee the lie,
Let seconds choose the field where you will die.

No legal surrogates, we win or die.
No wait upon the leaden pace of law.
The right will stand, the wrong will fallen lie
Expiring on the dewy grass at dawn,
And honour, satisfied, will not be scorned
When paid in liquid currency of blood.

Why does this hothead prate to me of blood?
He knows I've made a dozen like him die.
If he took back his lie he'd not be scorned.
A hasty word is no offense in law.
But if he drag me from my bed at dawn,
Forever breakfastless neath turf he'll lie.

I swear, for his unwelcome lie, he'll lie
And fertilize this green sward with his blood,
For this will be his last unhappy dawn.
At my unstained and practiced arm he'll die,
Victim of nature's universal law,
The strong survive to breed, the weak are scorned.

Alas my ancient name and title scorned,
Laid low by lucky lunge I dying lie,
Victim of pride, and hatred of the law.
Life seeps away in purple pool of blood,
Unnecessary, pointless, way to die,
Unheralded, un-breakfasted at dawn.

Honour is resurrected with the dawn,
My untried youth and courage no more scorned.
The first and last man I'll have caused to die.
Grass before breakfast, so my eggs don't lie
As vomit. God I hate the sight of blood!
Next time I'll trust the steamroller of law.

New civilized, we no more die, and lie
Empty, scorned by our peers abed at dawn,
But weakly substitute their law for blood.

THE GHAZAL

The ghazal is ancient, originating in Arabic poetry long before the birth of Islam. It is a poetic form with rhyming couplets and a refrain, each line sharing the same meter.

Unfortunately, being a man who never reads the complete instructions, I felt that that was all I needed to know to write one, so I missed this description of the content. "A ghazal may be understood as a poetic expression of both the pain of loss or separation and the beauty of love in spite of that pain."

Rather than throw out my painstakingly crafted first efforts, I include them here to show the folly of diving in before you have located the rocks! With "Wendie" I begin to scratch the surface of this beautiful form.

As a good example of a ghazal in English I recommend "Yasmin" by James Elroy Flecker.

GRAY FLANNEL TRAMP

Using the sobriquet, gray flannel tramp,
So no one will forget, gray flannel tramp,

He poses, poorly, as a sonneteer,
In trousered silhouette, gray flannel tramp.

Egged on by family, friends, and lady dear,
By childhood dreams beset, gray flannel tramp,

He slowly types cathartic poetry,
Attacking each dark bete, gray flannel tramp.

Philogynist, is moved to flattery,
Charming with a sonnet, gray flannel tramp.

If lacking inspiration he will hike
In sun or wind or wet, gray flannel tramp,

Musing till Thalia's sudden lightning strike,
His aging brain resets, gray flannel tramp.

YOUR RING OF FIRE

Tempestuous Pacific maid,
At rest within your ring of fire.

Welcome the hero unafraid,
Who dares to win your ring of fire.

With amour, horn and burnished blade,
Fearless strides through your ring of fire.

"Dast is kein Mann" with golden braid.
I force, sans sin, your ring of fire.

Cede softly, gently, undismayed,
To Paladin, your ring of fire.

WENDIE

What miles did I cycle just to see
A far off flash of golden hair, Wendie

How long I lingered in the lane alone
For one sweet moment we might share, Wendie

Recall our carol singing in the pub
I heard sweet trumpets fill the air, Wendie

Remember when we braved the Mendip cave
I thought that I had lost you there, Wendie

For you it was platonic never more
Which filled my heart with dark despair, Wendie

Now bittersweet I cherish memories
And letters in your hand my fair, Wendie

I know that I could find you on the web
But signs of age I could not bear, Wendie

Forever in my dreams you must remain
Young, beautiful, without a care, Wendie

THE OVILLEJO

The ovillejo is an old Spanish form popularized by Miguel de Cervantes (1547–1616). It was given a new lease on life in 2016 with the four hundreth anniversary of the deaths of Cervantes and Shakespeare.

This form has 10-lines comprised of four stanzas; 3 rhyming couplets and a quatrain.

The first line of each couplet is 8 syllables long and presents a question to which the second line responds in 3 to 4 syllables–either as an answer or an echo. The quatrain has an *abba* rhyme pattern and combines lines 2, 4, and 6 together as its final line.

I like the brevity of this form, but the difficulty lies in planning the answers to the questions to make sense in the final line. So I write the answers before the questions!!

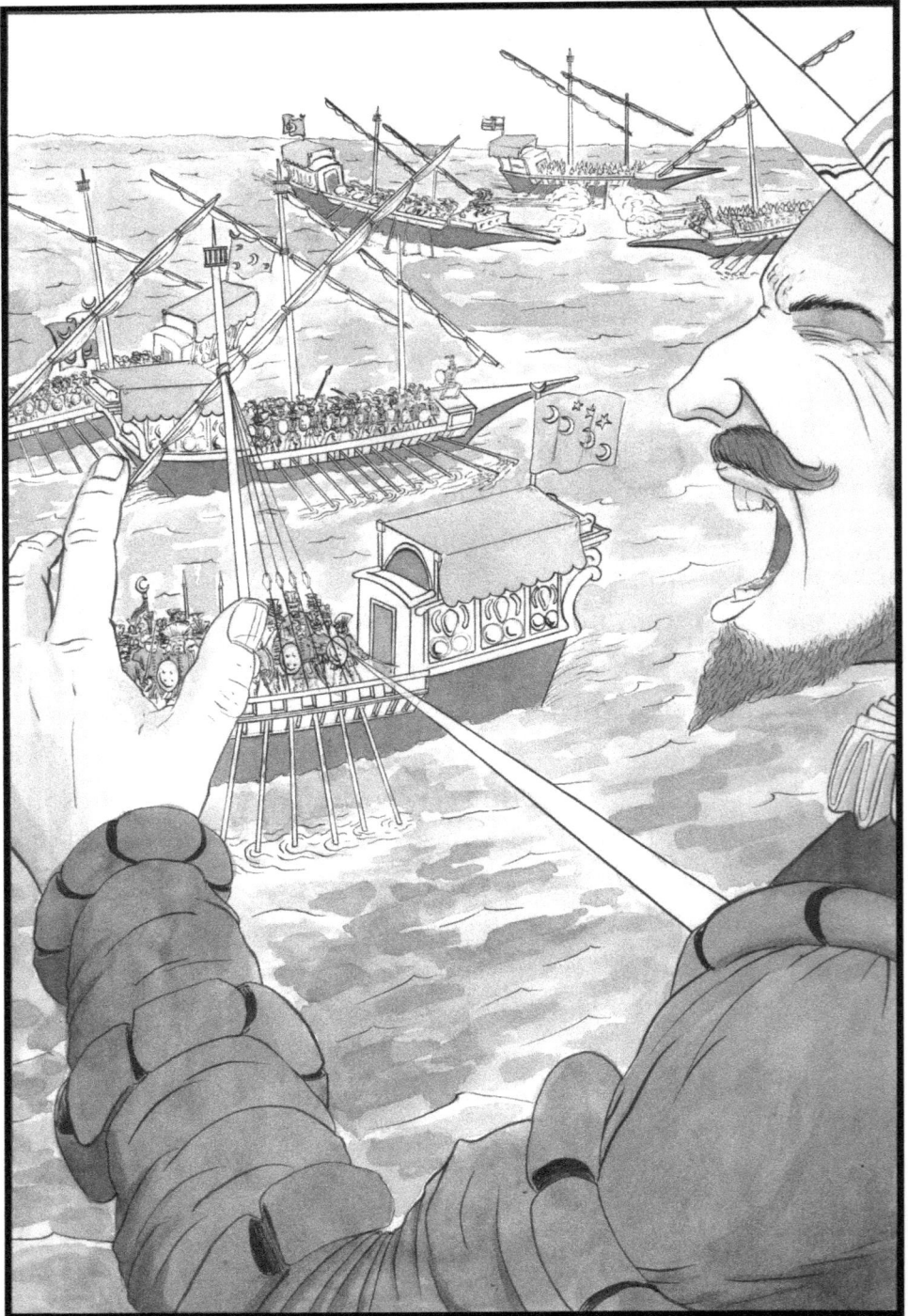

LEPANTO

Who is the foe that we must ban?
The Ottoman.

Where must we meet this Turkish foe?
At Lepanto.

What is the price to do them harm?
Cervantes arm.

Our battle plan worked like a charm,
But though their fleet was sunk or charred,
We almost lost La Mancha's bard.
The Ottoman at Lepanto, Cervantes arm.

BAROQUE BEAUTY

What drives a baroque pearl's selection?
Imperfection.

What makes *"Da capo"* heaven sent?
Embellishment.

What gives the fairest face its soul?
A velvet mole.

Though symmetry is beauty's goal,
To add a singularity
Can set imagination free.
Imperfection, embellishment, a velvet mole!

FROST FLOWERS

What flowers flourish without light?
Frost blossoms white.

When do fantastic fronds unfold?
In freezing cold.

How long does their stark beauty stun?
Till rise of sun.

No need for earth or cultivation,
Unrooted in their beds of glass,
They silent grow and quickly pass.
Frost blossoms white in freezing cold, till rise of sun.

CYWYDD

I find the Cywydd particularly hard to explain and it is really better suited to Welsh than English. However, even in English it has a special musical lilt to it. The following definition is from Webster:

A Cywydd is a Welsh verse form consisting of couplets of 7-syllable lines with varying cynghanedd and terminal rhyme that falls alternately on accented and on unaccented syllables. Cynghanedd is alliteration or alliteration and rhyme in any of the four patterns of cynghanedd.

If the reader is still interested in technicalities they can pursue their research via Wikipedia, unless they speak Welsh, in which case they probably know the answers.

My inspiration to try this form came from my other son who sent me a youtube link to "My first love was a plover": a modern Cywydd in English. Performed by Twm Morys.

THE HELL OF BELLS

Belfry bells small village hell
Pealing wake us feeling cruel
Triple bobs pull wrenching sobs
Grumblers shed their slumber robes
Pray the knell of pounding bell
Crack the Christian citadel
Empty pews the faithful snooze
Sabbath morn we'll scorn misuse
So your hymn sing soft not loud
Muted organ muffled crowd
Mutter Creed creep saved to house
Forty winks drinks for your spouse
Bury marry bless my child
Bells from hell serve for my shield

MIGRANTS

Migrants who mad tyrants flee,
Seeking aid, can safely be
Welcomed by our home grown sons,
Needy but not greedy ones.
Others, famine, fear, disease,
Crossing, tossing, no surcease,
Coat-less, float-less, in small boats,
Seeking, reaching, gentler coasts,
We'll help, will heal, provide them
Aid to evade their problem,
Assuming they'll assimilate,
Share our fate, participate,
But terrorists, on our lists,
Twisted e-mails, secret trysts,
Columns five, must not survive
To kill, assail us, where we live.

BEAVERS

Busy beavers back today
Signs on Houston's waterway
Chompers chewing cottonwood
Cripple creeks for fun or food
Seldom seen their tracks are there
Young trees gnawed beyond repair
Buffalo Bayou beavers build
Unseen lodges unfulfilled
Pretty soon the kits will come
Cutest babies under sun
Hardest working animals
Gold medalist of mammals
No more hunter gatherers
Trapping trading voyageurs
Hot top hats are out of style
Beaver coats no longer thrill
Scorned by skinning predators
Loathed by river landscapers
Sadly they are good to eat
Tastier than pork their meat
Cajuns crave their tubby tails
Pots and spices give them hell
God forbid they cause a flood
Then we'd bury them in mud

ANAGRAMMATICAL POEMS AND PUZZLES

There are two types of poem in this chapter. In the first section every line, or every other line, is an anagram of a person, place or literary work and in two of the poems the title is also an anagram.

In the next section are three puzzle poems with titles which are anagrams of a well known poet followed by a sonnet that gives clues to that poet's identity.

The answers can be found in the addendum.

SHAMES ARISTOTLE NOT

The "**sator**" mean is lost.
Time's loss, a heart not
Meant to, airless, host
Man's sore atheist lot.

"**Or mean**", that loses its
Name to hostile stars.
A lot these Romans sit,
Set in loathsome tars.

Time's ashen soot, Lars,
Toasts manliest hero.
Hail notes set to Mars,
Man less test "**Horatio**".

"SPEY RIVER" ANAGRAM

SIR PEVERY

the

PRIVY SEER

was an

EERY VP SIR

oh

YES REV RIP

you bane of every

REIVER SPY

while

I EVER SPRY

drank

VIPER'S RYE

you cried

ERR YE VIPS

then out

RIPS EVERY

laird's throat.

SREDNI VASHTAR
A DERVISH RANTS

Sand hit ravers
Ravish red ants.
Erst vain shard,
Darts his raven
Near trash, vids
Ishtar's red van.

Varnish treads
And shrive rats.
Stern, avid, rash,
Harvest drains,
Trash Ivan, Reds,
Avert rash Sind,
Rend Shiva star.

WE DROWN LIFE

We drown in mud the life blood of our youth,
In pointless struggles for unhallowed ground,
Cratered by shells, pocked, trenched, and pity proof,
Cruel man made obstacles advance confounds.
Where is the sweetness in a patriot's death,
For muddy inches of a foreign field.
Discard this ancient Latin shibboleth,
Which only draft proof geriatrics wield.
The flowers of a generation mowed
Down to make a million funeral wreaths.
Parents, wives and children, grief overflowed
For what! For when at last the sword was sheathed,
The "War to end all wars" did no such thing,
But gave new weapons and destroyed some Kings.

MANY HOT LADS

Many hot lads, from regiments far flung,
With basses deep, and tenor voices fine,
Have served their English masters, and have sung
Home sick songs of valleys and of mines.
And harp accompanied laments which show
The lack of English sensibility.
The Prince of Wales may be a dish, but no,
He's not a ruler they would wish to see.
Choirs, Eisteddfods, Rugby, play their part,
Diet, leeks, daffodils keep us apart,
And language boosts each rebel Cymric heart,
And yet their actors played a major part
In renaissance productions of the bard,
Did not go gentle to the knackers yard.

FEEL SO RANDY

I feel so randy that, despite the risk,
I ride, by moonlight, to my love tonight.
But first a shopping expedition brisk,
To steal some silver trinkets that, I hope, might
Look right well around her pretty neck and wrist.
I find that pistols easily persuade
Rich men, to give their daughter's arm a twist,
Deliver up her bracelets unafraid,
And on my handsome face bestow a kiss.
Yet, careless, blinded by repeat success,
Arrogant, the danger signs I miss,
Until I hear, O God to my distress,
Faint shot, but carried on soft evening air,
The warning death knell of my lover fair.

PRIMA AL QUADRATO

   While sitting in the Plaza in Santa Fe, dreaming away the long afternoons until the evening opera, I devised this poetic form to pass the time. It was so effective in this regard, that I spent most of my trip refining just one poem.

   I have called this form "Prima al Quadrato" meaning first squared, because it has eight lines and eight words per line with the first letter of each line and the first letter of each word within a line spelling out the title. After the first line the starting point begins to wrap around as the first letter of the line changes.

   While there are no rhymes or meter, the repetition of the title seems to have a mysterious power to create a unifying force. The challenge is to choose words that evoke images that lead the reader to fill in the blanks in the narrative.

THE PLAZA
(Santa Fe)

Take heart, each peon lends approving zeal, an
Hand extended, paw like, aged, zapped and tan,
Expressing pleasure, longing, at Zapata, and the hope
Peace long, and Zen, around the hills envelope
Los Alamos, zeitgeist at the Hopituh, expiring Pueblos,
Apache zealots, Anasazi, Taos horror, even papal loss.
Zephyrs at terpsichorean hands ease passions, liquid airs
Attend the hopeful emigres' pipes, lyres and zithers

RED MAIDS

Rest easy darling maids, as idyllic days slide
Elegantly down. Modest airs, impassion, disturb sun's rays,
Discompose my adoration. I dream secretly, red eyed,
Marvel at innocence displayed so recklessly each day.
Anon idly decide sequestration requires every defense man's
Intellect devise, so roues, evil, dangerous men afire,
Disarmed, spurned, routed, even driven mad, intran-
Sigent responses end. Death moderates all infamous desire.

THE ALAMO

Travis' heroic engagement against Lopez Anna, may offer
Hope, encouragement, and light, again, memories of Texian's
Efforts at loosening a mighty, oppressive, tyrant's hands.
As later, assailing Mexican oligarchs, tough Houston's essay,
Loosed against minions of Texas' hateful enemy, advancing
Alongside men of truest heart, energy and loyalty,
Mightily, our troops humbled, enfiladed, and, lambasted, all
Of those haughty enemies, and left a monument.

Addendum

The End of QEH

Queen Elizabeth's Hospital is a boy's boarding school in Bristol. It was founded in 1586 during the reign of Elizabeth I and remained a single sex school until a few years ago.

Grass before Breakfast

"Grass before Breakfast" is an old term for a duel.

Beavers and Buffalo Bayou

A sign on a trail along Buffalo Bayou in Houston, proclaims the presence of beavers. After some cursory research I found the evidence to be less than persuasive, but wrote the poem anyway.

The Pantoum "Buffalo Bayou" was written before the great flood of 2017 and should, perhaps be revised.

Shames Aristotle Not (Thomas Stearns Eliot)

Sator Square

The Sator Square or Rotas Square is a word square containing a Latin palindrome featuring the words SATOR AREPO TENET OPERA ROTAS, in this or in the reverse order, written in a square so that they may be read top-to-bottom, bottom-to-top, left-to-right, and right-to-left.

"Or Mean" refers to the "Golden Mean."

"Lars" is Lars Porsena the Etruscan king known for his war against the city of Rome. Who, refering to Horatio in Macaulay's poem "Horatio at the bridge" utters these lines;

"Heaven help him!" quoth Lars Porsena, "and bring him safe to shore;
For such a gallant feat of arms was never seen before."

Sredni Vashtar

"Sredni Vashtar" is a short story written by Saki (Hector Hugh Munro) between 1900 and 1911 and initially published in his book The Chronicles of Clovis.

We Drown Life (Wilfred Owen)

Wilfred Edward Salter Owen, MC was an English poet and soldier, one of the leading poets of the First World War. His war poetry on the horrors of trenches and gas warfare was heavily influenced by his mentor Siegfried Sassoon. Among his best-known works is "Dulce et Decorum est," which refers to "Dulce et decorum est pro patria mori," the ancient shibboleth in my poem.

Many Hot Lads (Dylan Thomas)

Dylan Marlais Thomas was a Welsh poet and writer whose works include the poems "Do not go gentle into that good night" and "And death shall have no dominion."

Feel So Randy (Alfred Noyes)

Alfred Noyes CBE was an English poet, short-story writer and playwright, best known for his ballads, "The Highwayman" and "The Barrel-Organ".

Red Maids (The Red Maids' School)

The Red Maids' School, founded in 1634, is a Bristol institution, and the oldest existing girls' school in the country.

Illustration Glossary

www.ingramcontent.com/pod-product-compliance
Lightning Source LLC
Chambersburg PA
CBHW032140040426
42449CB00005B/338